Brooke Lyne is a barrister at Landmark Chambers, specialising in property law. Her practice encompasses all areas of real property and landlord & tenant litigation both residential and commercial. She is the Assistant Editor of the Housing Law Encyclopedia and frequently writes journal articles for a number of different publications.

Brooke frequently acts for landlords and tenants in disputes involving disrepair and dilapidations. Such experience means she can provide insights into how the Homes (Fitness for Human Habitation) Act 2018 is likely to work in practice.

A Practical Guide to the Homes (Fitness for Human Habitation) Act 2018

A Practical Guide to the Homes (Fitness for Human Habitation) Act 2018

Brooke Lyne
Barrister, Landmark Chambers

Law Brief Publishing

Published 2019 by Law Brief Publishing, an imprint of Law Brief Publishing Ltd
30 The Parks
Minehead
Somerset
TA24 8BT

www.lawbriefpublishing.com

Paperback: 978-1-912687-48-0

ACKNOWLEDGEMENTS

I would like to thank all those friends and colleagues who have provided guidance and encouragement over the last few years. Life at the bar can be hard, but I am regularly astounded by the generosity of those around me.

Thank you to Tim Kevan and Garry Wright for providing the opportunity to write this book in the first place.

Finally, thank you, Adam, for your infinite patience and support.

Brooke Lyne
October 2019

CONTENTS

INTRODUCTION

1. This book is a short, practical guide to the Homes (Fitness for Human Habitation) Act 2018 ("the 2018 Act"), which is perhaps one of the most significant pieces of legislation in relation to housing conditions and disrepair of the twenty-first century so far. This book is designed as an accessible guide for legal practitioners, advisers and other professionals working in the private or social rental sectors. It may also be useful to landlords and tenants trying to navigate their respective rights and obligations under the new law.

2. The first chapter sets out the legislative terrain that existed prior to the 2018 Act and provides context about how it came to be passed. Understanding these matters is the best way to appreciate what the new law is trying to achieve. Thereafter the book looks at: what the 2018 Act does and how it is likely to be interpreted; what remedies will be available for tenants living in properties that are unfit for habitation and how damages are likely to be quantified; the practical and procedural matters to be considered when issuing a claim; and general hints and tips for landlords and tenants.

3. The law stated is as at 1 October 2019 and advisers should check for changes or updates.

CHAPTER ONE
DEFICIENCIES IN THE "OLD" LAW

1. The starting point is that there is no common law duty on landlords of residential premises to carry out repairs nor to ensure a dwelling is habitable[1] unless expressly provided for in the tenancy agreement. Furthermore, at common law there is no implied covenant that residential premises will be fit for human habitation.[2] In *Robbins v Jones* (1863) 15 CB Erle C.J. declared the following:

   "Fraud apart, there is no law against letting a tumbledown house, and the tenant's remedy is upon his contract, if any."

2. Lawyers have always had to start by considering the express terms of the lease to find out what – if any – repairing obligations fall on the landlord. There are any number of different types of repairing covenants that might appear in a tenancy agreement and the scope and extent of obligations will vary from one lease to the next. In practice, however, the express obligations on landlords in short tenancies tend to be drafted in terms that minimise the landlord's liability to carry out repairs.

3. The word "disrepair" is used generically by lawyers to describe claims or issues that involve problems with the state

1 See *Cavalier v Pope* [1906] A.C. 428.

2 There is an exception to this. If the property is furnished letting, then there is an implied term that the property will be fit for human habitation at the outset of the letting (*Smith v Marrable* (1843) 11 M&W 5). The obligation is not continuing and any unfitness that arises during the tenancy will not be actionable.

or condition of a property, but the legal definition of this term helps to demonstrate the deficiencies in the common law. Usually a landlord's repairing obligations under a short lease only arise if there is "disrepair", which means that the item or issue must be "out of repair" i.e. there has to be some deterioration from its previous condition. If it has always been in that condition or there is an "inherent defect" in the property then, ordinarily, the tenant will have no claim.

4. The gap in the law is acutely apparent if we consider the problem of condensation damp in residential premises. Condensation damp is rarely caused by "disrepair" to the dwelling (or to the building in which it is situated) but, instead, it is often caused by a design defect in the building which means that condensation damp forms because of an imbalance in the heating, insulation and ventilation in the dwelling. This form of damp, albeit horrible, and in some circumstances, dangerous for occupiers, is not usually actionable "disrepair". Moreover, the repairing covenant implied into short-term lettings by s.11 of the Landlord and Tenant Act 1985, does not provide a remedy for such condensation damp unless there is actual disrepair.[3]

The Extinction of s.8 Landlord and Tenant Act 1985

5. Section 8 of the Landlord and Tenant Act provided (it has been amended by the 2018 Act) that homes needed to be fit for human habitation. It implied two separate, absolute contractual terms into tenancies:

    - That the premises are fit for human habitation on the date of letting;

3 *Quick v Taff* [1986] Q.B. 809

- ○ That the premises will be kept fit for habitation, by the landlord, throughout the duration of the tenancy

6. Prior to the introduction of the 2018 Act, this provision only applied to properties at very low rents. The applicable rents were £80 rent per year in London and £52 per year elsewhere! As such, s.8 had become completely useless.

Other Provisions

7. Other provisions provided some recourse for tenants in poor standard housing prior to the commencement of the 2018 Act. This book does not attempt to cover them in any detail,[4] but by way of summary:

- Section 11, Landlord and Tenant Act 1985.

This provision imposes an implied term into secure and assured tenancies as well as all tenancies for a term of 7 years or less. The implied term imposed on the landlord is as follows:

> *"(a) to keep in repair the structure and exterior of the dwelling-house (including drains, gutters and external pipes),*
>
> *(b) to keep in repair and proper working order the installations in the dwelling-house for the supply of water, gas and electricity and for sanitation (including basins, sinks, baths and sanitary conveniences, but not other fixtures, fittings and appliances for making use of the supply of water, gas or electricity), and*

4 For that, readers should consult a practitioner text such as *Housing Conditions: Tenants Rights*, Luba, O'Donnell and Peaker; or *Dilapidations*, Dowding & Reynolds.

> *(c) to keep in repair and proper working order the installations in the dwelling-house for space heating and heating water."*

Under s.11(1A) the landlord is also responsible for other areas of the building over which she has an estate or interest. This means that a landlord who owns the whole building cannot escape liability if the cause of the disrepair originates from a part of the building outside of the tenant's demise. Ultimately, a tenant may bring a claim for breach of contract if the landlord fails to comply with her repairing obligations imposed by ss.11 and 11(1A).

- Section 4, Defective Premises Act 1972.

This provision imposes a duty on landlords to "take such care as is reasonable in all the circumstances" to ensure that occupiers "are reasonably safe from personal injury or from damage to their property caused by a relevant defect". This duty only applies when the landlord knew or ought to have known about the defect. It is possible for a tenant to bring a civil claim for breach of s.4.

- Occupiers Liability Act 1957

Under s.2(1) the "occupier" of land owes a common law duty to ensure that visitors are reasonably safe. A landlord who owns a whole building is treated as being the "occupier" of the retained common parts. This means that the landlord may be liable for injuries that occur as a result of the condition of communal parts of a building. A civil claim under this Act would have to be pursued against the landlord.

- Enforcement by local authority – Environmental Protection Act 1990

  This is not a civil remedy available to tenants, rather, it relates to the enforcement powers of local authorities. A local authority has powers and duties to take enforcement action against a landlord in circumstances where there is a "statutory nuisance". Tenants are able to invite the local authority to carry out a property inspection in the hope that the authority will take action to require the landlord to carry out works and/or remedy poor conditions.

Summary

8. The common law is inadequate when it comes to requiring landlords to ensure that residential properties are fit for occupation. There are several statutory provisions that provide some recourse for tenants and occupiers in poor housing, but overall these have provided inadequate protections.

CHAPTER TWO
CONTEXT TO THE ACT

1. Poor housing standards in England and Wales has been a long-standing issue, which has seen only gradual and piecemeal improvement over the last 20 years. Indeed, the English Housing Survey for 2016/17 showed that 27% of homes in the private rented sector did not meet the decent home standard.[1] Whilst the proportion of non-decent homes across the residential rental sector had steadily decreased from 2006, from 2014 progress had stagnated.[2] Perhaps this slow progress is best explained by the simple fact that housing standards is not a sexy topic for election manifestos and has rarely been considered "newsworthy" by tabloid press and other media outlets.

2. The Labour MP, Karen Buck has been a persistent campaigner for housing standards in the UK. In 2015 she attempted to use a Private Members Bill to update s.8 of the Landlord and Tenant Act 1985. She proposed to remove the low-rent limits so that s.8 would be applicable across the rental sector. Unfortunately, the Bill was talked out of Parliament at the Second Reading.

---

1 This is a non-statutory standard but, broadly speaking, a dwelling meets the decent home standard if it has no Category 1 hazards, is in a reasonable state of repair, has reasonably modern facilities and services; and provides a reasonable degree of thermal comfort.

2 The English Housing Survey 2016/17 recorded that, across all tenures, the proportion of non-decent homes declined steadily from 2006. From 2014, however, the proportion of non-decent homes had remained stable.

3. Attempts were then made to add Karen Buck's proposals to the Housing and Planning Bill 2015-16. Again, however, the amendments were voted down by the Government.

4. In 2017 Karen Buck got on the ballot again for a Private Members Bill and put her Bill forward one final time. By this point she had enlisted the support of two very good landlord & tenant lawyers (Justin Bates and Giles Peaker) to assist with drafting the proposed legislation. But there was no guarantee that the government would support her.

What had Changed?

5. On 14 June 2017 there was a fire in a 24-storey block of flats in North Kensington in the middle of the night. 72 people were killed. At the time of writing the public inquiry into the causes of the tragedy is ongoing. What is abundantly clear, however, is that the fire at Grenfell Tower caused a remarkable shift in the discourse surrounding housing standards. The political mood had altered, and politicians were willing to accept that legislation and regulation was necessary to provide greater protections to tenants in rented accommodation.

6. Karen Buck's Bill received cross-party support and received Royal Assent on 20 December 2018.

CHAPTER THREE WHAT DOES THE ACT DO?

1. The 2018 Act is relatively short. It amends sections 8-10 of the Landlord and Tenant Act 1985, and inserts new sections 9A, 9B and 9C.

Section 9A: the New Implied Term

2. The most important provision of the 2018 Act is the new s.9A(1)[1], which in England,[2] implies into any tenancy agreement a covenant by the landlord as follows:

> *"(1) In a lease to which this section applies of a dwelling in England (see section 9B), there is implied a covenant by the lessor that the dwelling—*
>
> > *(a) is fit for human habitation at the time the lease is granted or otherwise created or, if later, at the beginning of the term of the lease, and*
> >
> > *(b) will remain fit for human habitation during the term of the lease."*

3. These new provisions are pretty straightforward. From the outset of the tenancy a property will need to be fit for human habitation, and it must remain so throughout the period of that tenancy.

---

1 As introduced by s.1(3) of the 2018 Act.

2 The implied term applies to tenancies in England only. This is because similar provisions were introduced in Wales under Renting Homes (Wales) Act 2016.

4. Landlords cannot avoid or contract out of these implied terms, nor can any contractual penalty be levied on the tenant for relying on the covenant.[3]

Section 9B: When does it apply?

5. The 2018 Act came into force on 20 March 2019; three months after it received Royal Assent. At that point, the new amendments to the Landlord and Tenant Act 1985 came into force.

6. Section 9B provides that the new implied term applies immediately to new tenancies granted on or after the 20 March 2019. This includes "renewal" tenancies i.e. a new fixed term agreement granted by the same landlord to the same tenant on or after 20 March 2019.

7. The new implied term will apply to all periodic tenancies that were in existence before the commencement date, from on 20 March 2020 (12 months after commencement).

8. For tenancies that were originally for a fixed term, but became statutory periodic tenancies after 20 March 2019, then the new implied term will apply at that point.

9. It is important to remember that liability for breach of the implied term will only run from the date on which the new term is implied into an existing tenancy. So, the earliest[4] date from which any damages will be calculated is the date when

---

3 Section 9A(4), Landlord and Tenant Act 1985.

4 Remember, liability only starts to run from the date on which the landlord has had knowledge of the unfitness and has failed to remedy it within a reasonable time. See para 38 below.

new term was implied, even if the items of "unfitness" were pre-existing.

When Does the Implied Term Apply?

Type of tenancy	Date of grant	When does the implied term apply?
Fixed term granted for 2 years	Before 20 March 2019	The implied term does not apply until a new tenancy arises (either a new fixed term or a statutory periodic tenancy)
New fixed term or periodic granted	On or after 20 March 2019	Immediately
Existing periodic tenancy (e.g. secure or assured periodic)	Before 20 March 2019	20 March 2020
Fixed term that becomes statutory periodic tenancy	Fixed term expires on or after 20 March 2019	Term applies as soon as the statutory periodic tenancy arises.

What Types of Tenancy? (sections 9B, 9C, 13 and 14)

10. The relevant provisions that set out the types of tenancies to which the new implied term applies are: ss. 9B, 9C, 13 and 14 of the Landlord and Tenant Act 1985. They provide as follows:

Section 9B

"(1) Section 9A applies to a lease under which a dwelling is ***let wholly or mainly for human habitation*** *if either of the following applies—*

(a) the ***lease is for a term of less than 7 years****, or*

(b) the lease is of a kind mentioned in subsection (1A) or (1AB) of section 13 (leases to which section 11 applies: secure, assured or introductory tenancies for fixed term of 7 years or more).

This is subject as follows.

(2) Section 9A does not apply to any lease of a kind mentioned in section 14 (exceptions for leases to which section 11 applies).

(3) Except as mentioned in subsections (4), (5) and (6), section 9A does not apply to a lease granted—

(a) before the commencement date, or

(b) on or after that date in pursuance of an agreement entered into, or an order of a court made, before the commencement date.

(4) Section 9A applies to a periodic or secure tenancy that is in existence on the commencement date, but in the case of any such tenancy the covenant implied by that section has effect in the following way—

(a) subsection (1)(a) of that section has effect as if the reference to the later of the times there mentioned were a reference to the time that begins at the end of the period

of 12 months beginning with the commencement date, and

(b) subsection (1)(b) of that section has effect only in respect of times falling after the end of that 12-month period.

(5) Section 9A applies to a periodic or secure tenancy that comes into existence after the commencement date on expiry of a term of a lease granted before that date.

(6) Section 9A applies to a lease for a fixed term which—

(a) is granted or renewed before the commencement date, and

(b) is renewed for a further fixed term on or after that date,

and for this purpose the renewal on or after the commencement date is to be treated as a grant of the lease on or after that date.

(7) For the purposes of subsection (1) it is immaterial—

(a) whether the dwelling is to be occupied under the lease or under an inferior lease derived out of it, or

(b) that the lease also demises other property (which may consist of or include one or more other dwellings).

(8) In determining for the purposes of subsection (1)(a) whether a lease is for a term of less than 7 years—

(a) any part of the term falling before the grant or creation is to be ignored and the lease is to be treated as a lease for a term commencing with the grant or creation;

(b) a lease which is determinable at the option of the lessor before the expiry of 7 years from the commencement of the term is to be treated as a lease for a term of less than 7 years;

(c) a lease (other than one to which paragraph (b) applies) is not to be treated as a lease for a term of less than 7 years if it confers on the lessee an option for renewal for a term which, together with the original term, amounts to 7 years or more.

(9) In this section—

"the commencement date" means the date on which the Homes (Fitness for Human Habitation) Act 2018 comes into force;

"lease", "lessee" and "lessor" have the same meanings as in section 9A;

"secure tenancy" has the meaning given by section 79 of the Housing Act 1985.

"a lease under which a dwelling is let wholly or mainly for human habitation" (9B(1)) and either

(a) the lease is for a term of less than 7 years, or

(b) secure, assured or introductory tenancies for fixed term of 7 years or more"

Section 9C

"(1) This section applies where under a contract of employment of a worker employed in agriculture—

(a) the provision of a dwelling for the worker's occupation forms part of the worker's remuneration, and

(b) the provisions of section 9A (implied term as to fitness for human habitation of dwellings in England) are inapplicable by reason only of the dwelling not being let to the worker.

(2) There is implied as part of the contract of employment (in spite of any stipulation to the contrary) a term having the same effect as the covenant that would be implied by section 9A if the dwelling were let by a lease to which that section applies.

(3) The provisions of section 9A apply accordingly—

(a) with the substitution of "employer" and "employee" for "lessor" and "lessee", and

(b) with such other modifications as may be necessary.

(4) This section does not affect—

(a) any obligation of a person other than the employer to repair a dwelling to which the covenant implied by section 9A applies by virtue of this section, or

(b) any remedy for enforcing such an obligation."

Section 13(1A) and (1B):

"(1A) Section 11 also applies to a lease of a dwelling-house in England granted on or after the day on which section 166 of the Localism Act 2011 came into force which is—

(a) a ***secure tenancy for a fixed term of seven years or more*** *granted by a person within section 80(1) of the Housing Act 1985 (secure tenancies: the landlord condition), or*

(b) an ***assured tenancy for a fixed term of seven years*** *or more that—*

(i) is not a shared ownership lease, and

(ii) is granted by a private registered provider of social housing.

(1B) In subsection (1A)—

"assured tenancy" has the same meaning as in Part 1 of the Housing Act 1988;

"secure tenancy" has the meaning given by section 79 of the Housing Act 1985; and

"shared ownership lease" means a lease—

(a) granted on payment of a premium calculated by reference to a percentage of the value of the dwelling-house or of the cost of providing it, or

(b) under which the lessee (or the lessee's personal representatives) will or may be entitled to a sum calculated by reference, directly or indirectly, to the value of the dwelling-house."

Section 14

"(1) Section 11 (repairing obligations) does not apply to a new lease granted to an existing tenant, or to a former tenant still in possession, if the previous lease was not a lease

to which section 11 applied (and, in the case of a lease granted before 24th October 1961, would not have been if it had been granted on or after that date).

(2) In subsection (1)—

"existing tenant" means a person who is when, or immediately before, the new lease is granted, the lessee under another lease of the dwelling-house;

"former tenant still in possession" means a person who—

> *(a) was the lessee under another lease of the dwelling-house which terminated at some time before the new lease was granted, and*
>
> *(b) between the termination of that other lease and the grant of the new lease was continuously in possession of the dwelling-house or of the rents and profits of the dwelling-house; and*

"the previous lease" means the other lease referred to in the above definitions.

(3) Section 11 does not apply to a lease of a dwelling-house which is a tenancy of an agricultural holding within the meaning of the Agricultural Holdings Act 1986 and in relation to which that Act applies or to a farm business tenancy within the meaning of the Agricultural Tenancies Act 1995.

(4) Section 11 does not apply to a lease granted on or after 3rd October 1980 to—

a local authority,

a National Park authority,

a new town corporation,

an urban development corporation,

a Mayoral development corporation,

the Development Board for Rural Wales,

a non-profit registered provider of social housing,

a registered social landlord,

a co-operative housing association,

an educational institution or other body specified, or of a class specified, by regulations under section 8 of the Rent Act 1977 or paragraph 8 of Schedule 1 to the Housing Act 1988 (bodies making student lettings), or

a housing action trust established under Part III of the Housing Act 1988

(5) Section 11 does not apply to a lease granted on or after 3rd October 1980 to—

(a) Her Majesty in right of the Crown (unless the lease is under the management of the Crown Estate Commissioners), or

(b) a government department or a person holding in trust for Her Majesty for the purposes of a government department."

11. These sections are relatively clunky and hard to follow. In reality, however, the new provisions apply (or will apply) to most residential tenancies in England as long as it is "a dwelling that is let wholly or mainly for human habitation". The following types of tenancy are covered:

    - Secure tenancies
    - Introductory tenancies
    - Assured tenancies
    - Assured shorthold tenancies
    - Protected tenancies under the Rent Act 1977
    - Licences of accommodation tied to agricultural employment

12. There are, of course, exceptions. The new implied term will not apply to these types of letting (this is not an exhaustive list):

    - Non-residential tenancies
    - Long leases
    - Licences
    - Tenancies of agricultural holdings
    - Leases granted by the Crown or a government department, held on trust for Her Majesty

What is the Extent of the Obligation?

13. The obligation extends to the "dwelling" itself, whether it be a room, flat or house that has been demised to the tenant. If the dwelling forms part of a building, so for example, a flat in a block, or a room in a house in multiple occupation, then the obligation extends to all parts of the building in which the landlord has an estate or interest.

14. This provision parallels s.11(1A) of the Landlord and tenant Act 1985, which similarly puts obligations on a landlord who owns other parts of the building. So, where a landlord owns a block of flats, the tenant has a cause of action where unfitness arises from the common parts, or the retained parts. So, for example, if there is a leak into a flat from the roof that is causing a property to be unfit for human habitation, if the landlord owns the whole building, then he will be required to fix the leak.

Section 10: What Does "Unfitness for Human Habitation" Actually Mean?

15. Perhaps the most obvious, and yet difficult question that arises in relation to the 2018 Act is the meaning of the central concept of "unfitness for human habitation". The new s.10[5] of the 1985 Act provides as follows:

> *"(1) In determining for the purposes of this Act whether a house or dwelling is unfit for human habitation, regard shall be had to its condition in respect of the following matters—*

5 As amended by s.4, 2018 Act.

> *repair, stability, freedom from damp, internal arrangement, natural lighting, ventilation, water supply, drainage and sanitary conveniences, facilities for preparation and cooking of food and for the disposal of waste water in relation to a dwelling in England, any prescribed hazard;...*

> *and the house or dwelling shall be regarded as unfit for human habitation if, and only if, it is so far defective in one or more of those matters that* ***it is not reasonably suitable for occupation in that condition.***"

> .....

> *"(2) In subsection (1) "prescribed hazard" means any matter or circumstance amounting to a hazard for the time being prescribed in regulations made by the Secretary of State under section 2 of the Housing Act 2004.*

> *(3) The definition of "hazard" in section 2(1) of the Housing Act 2004 applies for the purposes of subsection (2) as though the reference to a potential occupier were omitted."*

16. So, in deciding whether a property is unfit, regard shall be had to the factors that are listed in subsection (1). These are the same factors as those listed under s.8, Landlord and Tenant Act 1985, save for the addition of "prescribed hazard".

"Prescribed hazard"

17. As per subsection (2), "prescribed hazard" is defined by reference to regulations made under the Housing Act 2004. At the time of writing the relevant regulations are the Housing Health and Safety Rating System (England) Regulations

2005 (SI 3208) ("HHSRS"). If these are ever amended or updated, then the new or amended regulations will apply. The HHSRS is an evaluation tool used by local authorities to identify, assess and protect[6] against potential risks and hazards to health and safety in residential accommodation. For present purposes, it is a readily available list of hazards that the court will consider when assessing fitness for human habitation.

18. Schedule 1 of the 2005 regulations sets out what the 29 different types of hazard are as follows:

"Damp and mould growth

1. Exposure to house dust mites, damp, mould or fungal growths.

Excess cold

2. Exposure to low temperatures.

Excess heat

3. Exposure to high temperatures.

Asbestos and MMF

4. Exposure to asbestos fibres or manufactured mineral fibres.

Biocides

5. Exposure to chemicals used to treat timber and mould growth.

---

6 Local authorities have powers under the Housing Act 2004 to carry out inspections of residential accommodation and to service enforcement notices in circumstances where prescribed hazards are identified.

Carbon monoxide and fuel combustion products

6. Exposure to—

(a) carbon monoxide;

(b) nitrogen dioxide;

(c) sulphur dioxide and smoke.

Lead

7. The ingestion of lead.

Radiation

8. Exposure to radiation.

Uncombusted fuel gas

9. Exposure to uncombusted fuel gas.

Volatile organic compounds

10. Exposure to volatile organic compounds.

Crowding and space

11. A lack of adequate space for living and sleeping.

Entry by intruders

12. Difficulties in keeping the dwelling or HMO secure against unauthorised entry.

Lighting

13. A lack of adequate lighting.

Noise

14. Exposure to noise.

Domestic hygiene, pests and refuse

15. -- (1) Poor design, layout or construction such that the dwelling or HMO cannot readily be kept clean.

(2) Exposure to pests.

(3) An inadequate provision for the hygienic storage and disposal of household waste.

Food safety

16. An inadequate provision of facilities for the storage, preparation and cooking of food.

Personal hygiene, sanitation and drainage

17. An inadequate provision of—

(a) facilities for maintaining good personal hygiene;

(b) sanitation and drainage.

Water supply

18. An inadequate supply of water free from contamination, for drinking and other domestic purposes.

Falls associated with baths etc

19. Falls associated with toilets, baths, showers or other washing facilities.

Falling on level surfaces etc

20. Falling on any level surface or falling between surfaces where the change in level is less than 300 millimetres.

Falling on stairs etc

21. Falling on stairs, steps or ramps where the change in level is 300 millimetres or more.

Falling between levels

22. Falling between levels where the difference in levels is 300 millimetres or more.

Electrical hazards

23. Exposure to electricity.

Fire

24. Exposure to uncontrolled fire and associated smoke.

Flames, hot surfaces etc

25. Contact with—

(a) controlled fire or flames;

(b) hot objects, liquid or vapours.

Collision and entrapment

26. Collision with, or entrapment of body parts in, doors, windows or other architectural features.

Explosions

27. An explosion at the dwelling or HMO.

Position and operability of amenities etc

28. The position, location and operability of amenities, fittings and equipment.

Structural collapse and falling elements

29. The collapse of the whole or part of the dwelling or HMO."

19. Of course, some of these listed items are more likely to occur than others (thankfully, the occurrence of hazardous levels of radiation in disrepair cases tend to be relatively rare). Whilst any of these factors will be automatically taken into account if they arise, it is not *necessary* for any of them to be present for a property to be unfit for human habitation. Moreover, it is not necessary that a claimant has involved the local authority at all in order to issue a claim.

20. The question for the court is: whether the dwelling is 'not reasonably suitable for occupation in that condition'?

21. This test appears to be an objective one. One of the key issues that is likely to be the subject of judicial consideration is the relevance, or perhaps irrelevance, of the circumstances of the *particular occupier*. For example, a property that contains damp and mould is likely to have a more serious impact on an occupier who suffers from severe asthma. The threshold of "unfitness" for some occupiers will be higher or lower than others. Will the courts assess fitness according the circumstances of that particular occupier or according to an

objective standard; say the average or perhaps reasonable occupier?

22. A subjective approach would lead to uncertainty and would impose unrealistic and variable expectations on landlords. For example, if a landlord is required to ensure that the property is fit for habitation by a particular occupier then she will surely need to have knowledge of the health and condition of all persons living in the accommodation at all times. As a result, the writer envisages[7] that the courts will consider whether the property is fit for habitation by **all classes of person that might reasonably be expected to occupy it**. Such an approach has been taken in cases under the Defective Premises Act 1972.[8]

The Common Law Definition

23. How the courts will interpret the meaning of "unfitness for human habitation" under the new Act will be the subject of litigation. Nonetheless, this central concept is not new at all and old case law is likely to be of some assistance.

Wilson v Finch Hatton (1877) 2 Ex.D 336

24. This case of involved the letting of a furnished house in Belgravia. The tenant was a wealthy woman who arrived at the house with her servants, horses and luggage but would not occupy it owing to a foul smell. It transpired that the old brick drains were out of repair. There was a cesspool under the pantry, and a considerable amount of stagnant sewage was under the basement floor causing the odour. The court

7 Though, of course, at the time of writing there are no reported decisions on how the 2018 Act will be interpreted.

8 See *Rendlesham Estates Plc v Barr Ltd* [2014] EWHC 3968.

was satisfied that the property was unfit for human habitation in that condition.

Smith v Marrable (1843) 11 M. & W. 5

25. This case concerned the letting of a furnished house in Brighton. The house was infested with bugs, so after less than a week the tenant moved his family to live somewhere else. The landlord sought unpaid charges due under the tenancy. The court held that the charges were not recoverable because the landlord was in breach of an implied term (because it was a furnished that the property) that the property would be fit for habitation at the outset of the letting. The infestation of bugs was sufficient to amount to "unfitness" for human habitation.

Collins v Hopkins [1923] 2 KB 617

26. The defendant let to the claimant a furnished property in St Albans, which was to be occupied by Mr Collins, his wife, his daughter and servants. A day after they moved in Mr Collins discovered that the landlord's husband, who was suffering from Tuberculosis, had recently occupied the property but had been taken to Switzerland for treatment. Concerned about the possibility of contracting the disease, Mr Collins and his family moved out immediately. He argued that he was entitled to repudiate the agreement because the landlord was in breach of the implied covenant (this was a furnished letting so such a covenant is implied) that the property would be fit for human habitation at the outset. The presence, or potential presence, of infectious bacteria made the property unfit for occupation. The court agreed.

27. Macardi J said this at [620-622]:

> *"What is the meaning of "fit for habitation"? The meaning of the phrase must vary with the circumstances to which it is applied. In the case of unclean furniture or defective drains or a nuisance by vermin the matter is not, as a rule, one of difficulty. The eye or the nostrils can detect the fault and measure its extent. But in the case of a house lately occupied by a person suffering from an infectious disease, the eye and other senses are of no avail. The bacilli of infection are not apparent to the eye. Yet a peril is none the less grave because it is hidden.*
>
> *[...]*
>
> *In my view the question in such a case as the present is this: Was there an actual and appreciable risk to the tenant, his family or household, by entering and occupying the house in which the infectious disorder had occurred? If the risk be serious, no one, I think, could doubt that the tenant may renounce. But in dealing with bacilli which may mean illness and death, I think further that an appreciable measure of actual risk justifies the tenant in throwing up his contract. A man should not be called on to expose his wife and children, household or himself to peril.*
>
> *Amongst the matters to be considered are the nature of the disease; the degree and persistence of its infectivity; the date when the sufferer resided in the house; the steps taken to prevent risk of infection and the like."*

Edwards v Etherington (1825) 7 Dow. & Ry K.B. 117.

28. This case involved a letting where the premises was structurally unsafe owing to a party wall in the basement, which

had been partially removed. Perhaps, unsurprisingly, the court accepted that the property was unfit for habitation.

Bole v Huntsbuild Limited [2009] EWCA Civ 1146

29. This case concerned the meaning and application of section 1, Defective Premises Act 1972, which (amongst other things) imposes the following duties on house builders:

> *"(1) A person taking on work for or in connection with the provision of a dwelling (whether the dwelling is provided by the erection or by the conversion or enlargement of a building) owes a duty—*
>
> *(a) if the dwelling is provided to the order of any person, to that person; and*
>
> *(b) without prejudice to paragraph (a) above, to every person who acquires an interest (whether legal or equitable) in the dwelling;*
>
> *to see that the work which he takes on is done in a workmanlike or, as the case may be, professional manner, with proper materials and so that as regards that work the* ***dwelling will be fit for habitation when completed.****"*

30. There was no dispute that the structural engineers owed this duty under s.1, DPA 1972. The claimants alleged that the defendants were in breach of their duty because the foundations of the property had been badly designed and had caused cracking and other defects inside the property. The defendants denied that these defects made the property unfit for human habitation. On first instance the judge was satisfied that the property was unfit for human habitation.

31. On appeal the defendants argued that the judge had been wrong because:

   (a) he incorrectly considered the question whether the dwelling was suitable for its "purpose" rather than whether it was unfit for habitation;

   (b) he took into account an irrelevant consideration, namely the duration of the remedial works and the fact that the claimants would have to leave the dwelling for about 12 months while the works were being carried out; and

   (c) the judge failed to consider each of the defects relied on by the claimants, and decide whether individually, or taken in conjunction with other defects, they rendered the dwelling unfit for habitation.

32. The Court of Appeal rejected all of these arguments. On the first issue the court was unpersuaded that the judge had applied the incorrect test – there had been no material error in the Judge's reasoning. On the second issue, Dyson LJ concluded as follows:

> *"I cannot accept that the fact that it would be necessary for the claimants to vacate the dwelling for a substantial period during the carrying out of the remedial works is irrelevant. In some cases, it may be irrelevant. It may be that in the rather unrealistic example given by Mr Hussain to illustrate his point, the fact that the owners would have to vacate the dwelling for 12 months during the carrying out of the remedial works would be irrelevant to the question whether the defects render the dwelling unfit for habitation. It will always depend on the facts of the particular case. But in a case where the defect is fundamental to the stability of the*

dwelling, and does not raise a merely cosmetic or stylistic issue, the fact that it is necessary to vacate for a long period, while the remedial work carried out, is likely to be highly material to whether the defect renders the dwelling unfit for habitation. In my judgment, the judge was not only entitled, but right to regard the fact that it would be necessary for the claimants to vacate for about 12 months during the remedial works, as material. Mr Hussain has cited no authority in support of the proposition that the duration of the remedial works, and the fact that it would be necessary for the claimants to vacate the dwelling while the remedial works are carried out, is necessarily and in every case, irrelevant. In my judgment, in many cases it will be a highly relevant indicator of whether the defect or defects have rendered the dwelling unfit for habitation."

33. On the third issue, again the defendant's approach was rejected and at [34] Dyson LJ provided some guidance as to how the court ought to approach the question of unfitness of a dwelling "as a whole":

> *"The judge was not obliged to approach the question of whether there had been a breach of Section 1 in this case, by considering each defect individually and asking whether that defect, or indeed, that defect taken in conjunction with other individual defects, rendered the dwelling unfit for habitation. He was entitled to ask himself whether the dwelling as a whole was unfit for habitation. The judge found that it suffered from a fundamental defect, namely inadequate foundations. There was what the judge described at paragraph 170 as "widespread cracking" which was the result of ground heave, which in turn was attributable to the inadequacy of the foundations. Some cracks, when viewed as individual cracks, were more serious than others.*

> *The cracks referred to in paragraphs 158 to 163 were, of themselves, quite serious and even when considered on their own, arguably rendered the dwelling unfit for habitation. Other cracks and defects were in themselves less serious, nevertheless, all the defects, including all the cracks as well as warped doors, et cetera, were the result of the ground heave and ultimately inadequate foundations. In reaching his conclusion that the dwelling was unfit for habitation, the judge took into account all the defects and the fact that they were caused by a fundamental defect: namely, the inadequacy of the foundations."*

Harrison v Shepherd Homes Ltd [2011] EWHC 1811

34. This case was, similarly, concerned with "fitness for habitation" in the context of a claim under the Defective Premises Act 1972. The claimants were the owners of houses who sought damages from the construction company alleging that the houses had been unfit for habitation upon completion. Walls inside the houses suffered extensive cracking as a result of problems with the foundations. The Judge considered the principles said out in *Bole v Huntsbuild Limited* [2009] EWCA Civ 1146 and accepted that the houses were unfit for habitation as follows at [745]:

> *"It was common ground that the question of whether a dwelling is fit for habitation is one of fact and degree. In this case there are defects in the foundations which have caused, as set out below, only cosmetic defects in the properties, that is category 1 defects under the definition in BRE Digest 241. This is not a case where the defects have caused category 4 defects as in Bole It is not a case where significant damage is likely. However, as the claimants submit, the judgment of Dyson L.J. at [30] would indicate that security*

is one of the criteria for fitness for habitation and at [29] there was a reference to inconvenience.

In this case there are essentially two aspects: the defective piles and the damage caused to the properties by the defective piles. Whilst I do not consider that the damage to the properties has rendered them unfit for habitation, on balance, I am persuaded that any significant defects in foundations are properly matters which could be said to give rise to a lack of fitness for habitation. On that basis I would conclude that this is a case where the properties are, to that extent, not fit for habitation.

I therefore find that the defects in this case were caused by the foundation work not being done in a workmanlike or professional manner so that as regards that work the properties were not fit for habitation when completed."

Rendlesham Estates Plc v Barr Ltd [2014] EWHC 3968

35. Again, this case was brought under the Defective Premises Act 1972. The claim was brought on behalf of 120 leaseholders from two apartment blocks who sought damages from the developer that had built the blocks. Soon after completion problems had developed including, issues with the intercom system, leaks from walkways, leaks from balconies and showers, and mould and damp growth. The claimants alleged that their apartments were unfit for human habitation when completed.

36. The judge considered the meaning of "fitness for habitation" (relying upon *Bole v Huntsbuild Limited* [2009] EWCA Civ 1146 and *Harrison v Shepherd Homes Ltd* [2011] EWHC 1811) and made the following observations:

"68 In my judgment, for a dwelling to be fit for habitation within the meaning of the Act, it must, on completion (without any remedial works being carried out): (a) be capable of occupation for a reasonable time without risk to the health or safety of the occupants: where a dwelling is or is part of a newly constructed building, what is a reasonable time will be a question of fact (it may or may not be as long as the design life of the building); and (b) be capable of occupation for a reasonable time without undue inconvenience or discomfort to the occupants.

[...]

73 It must also follow, as a matter of principle, that ***the dwelling should be fit for habitation by all the classes of people who might reasonably be expected to occupy it:*** *this may include, for example, pregnant women, babies and children, and those who suffer from common ailments or allergies, such as asthma or hay fever. (I do not consider here the position of those with particularly severe disabilities, such as the blind or those who are severely physically disabled. Such issues do not arise in this case and so I prefer to say nothing more about them.)*

[...]

76 In deciding whether a dwelling is fit for habitation where there is more than one defect it is not right to consider each of the defects in isolation. It is appropriate to consider whether the dwelling as a whole was unfit for habitation: see the Bole case.

[...]

> *79 So far as mould and damp is concerned, I have discussed the consequences of this in more detail in Appendix E in the context of the external walls. I have no doubt that the presence of mould and damp in living rooms or bedrooms, if persistent and more than minor, renders an apartment unfit for habitation. Damp living conditions are well known to pose a risk to health, and there is evidence from some witnesses of actual risks to health or concern about the potential risk, either to themselves or children.*

37. The extent to which these cases will be followed under the 2018 Act is yet to be seen. Nonetheless, for lawyers looking to advise their clients on the meaning of "fitness for human habitation", these cases are a helpful starting point.

What Notice is Required?

The demised premises

38. A significant about of time in disrepair trials is spent dealing with the "I didn't know!" argument put forward by a landlord who insists that the tenant has never mentioned the issues now complained of. This means that lawyers spend lots of time rifling through repair records and emails to see whether the tenants did notify their landlord about issues or not.

39. At common law[9] there is a term implied into tenancy agreements that a landlord's repairing obligations *within demised premises* will only arise after:

    (a) she has been put on notice or has knowledge of the disrepair;

---

9 See *O'Brien v Robinson* [1973] AC 912.

(b) she failed to carry out the repair within a reasonable period of time after notice is given.

40. This requirement for notice applies equally to statutory repairing obligations as well as express obligations provided in a tenancy agreement. **The writer considers that this common law requirement for notice to be given will almost certainly apply to the 2018 Act.**

41. The tenant is not obliged to explain the extent or source of disrepair but must give the landlord such notice as would place a reasonable landlord on inquiry.[10] The courts adopt a sensible approach. If, for example, the issue is an obvious problem, perhaps a burst pipe or leak coming through the ceiling, then a mere property inspection by landlord or her agent is likely to be enough to constitute good notice. If the issue is less obvious, perhaps a hole in the roof that can only be identified if you access the loft, then the tenant will need to go further to draw it to the landlord's attention.

42. A landlord may have "knowledge" of disrepair by any number of different methods. The most obvious is when the tenant tells the landlord directly. Of course, written evidence and records are the most prudent way to ensure that the tenant can prove that they have given the requisite notice. A landlord may be deemed to have knowledge when disrepair has been brought to the attention of her agents e.g. an employee; workman or other person who has authority to receive complaints on the landlord's behalf.[11] Service of a statutory notice by a local authority has been held to be sufficient to establish that the landlord had knowledge of

---

10 *Dinefwr Borough Council v Jones* [1987] 19 H.L.R. 445

11 See, for example, *Sheldon v West Bromwich Corporation* (1984) 13 HLR 23

disrepair.[12] The landlord may have constructive knowledge if there is a problem at the outset of the tenancy and a property inspection is carried out beforehand.

Retained areas

43. The position in relation to communal areas is slightly different. The rule requiring notice does not apply in relation to areas of the premises that are retained by the landlord and over which she has repairing obligations. In such a case, the landlord is liable for breach of covenant as and when a disrepair occurs and whether she knows about it or not.[13] Further, she does not have a reasonable period of time to remedy the defect before liability arises.

44. Of course, the position on notice for retained areas puts absentee landlords in a difficult situation – regular checks as to the condition of communal areas is very important. The most sensible course is for a tenant to notify the landlord about a defect in the communal areas as soon as possible because a failure to do so could result in a reduction in the amount of damages awarded because of the failure to mitigate loss.[14]

Access

45. Of course, in order to ensure a property is fit for human habitation a landlord needs to be allowed to access it. Any lawyer that has been involved in disrepair cases will tell you that

---

12 *McGreal v Wake* (1984) 13 HLR 107

13 Most recently confirmed by the Supreme Court in *Edwards v Kumarasamy* [2016] UKSC 40

14 *Minchburn v Peck* (1988) 20 HLR 392

"access" is frequently a point of contention between landlords and tenants before and during proceedings. Tenants often get fed up with landlords and agents demanding access at the last minute when they have work or other commitments. Landlords frequently complain that tenants refuse access unreasonably and make it impossible to get contractors to resolve issues of disrepair. These same issues will continue under the 2018 Act, which makes express provision for rights of access for landlords.

46. Subsections 9A(7) and (8) provide as follows:

> *"(7) In a lease to which this section applies of a dwelling in England, there is also implied a covenant by the lessee that the lessor, or a person authorised in writing by the lessor, may enter the dwelling for the purpose of viewing its condition and state of repair.*
>
> *(8) The covenant implied by subsection (7) requires entry to the dwelling to be permitted—*
>
> > *(a) only at reasonable times of the day, and*
> >
> > *(b) only if at least 24 hours' notice in writing has been given to the occupier of the dwelling."*

47. So, subsection (7) implies a covenant that the landlord, or a person authorised by the landlord, may enter the dwelling for the purpose of viewing its condition and state of repair. Subsection (8) provides that entry is to be provided only at reasonable times of the day and when 24 hours written notice.

Exceptions to Liability

48. As with old-style disrepair cases, there are defences that may be raised by landlords to avoid liability. Indeed, the 2018 Act creates a number of statutory exceptions that may mean that a landlord avoids liability.

Behaving in a tenant-like manner/ tenant's breach of covenant

49. A landlord will not be responsible for unfitness in a property that has been caused by the tenant's failure to behave in a "tenant-like manner",[15] or that results from the tenant's breach of covenant.[16]

50. The requirement to behave in a "tenant-like manner" is likely to be interpreted in accordance with the common law[17] and in light of the fact and circumstances of each case.

51. There are some obvious circumstances where disputes about the behaviour of tenants is likely to come up. For example, consider a situation where there is damp and mould inside a property as a result of condensation. In some instances, the tenant's behaviour in failing to open windows or turn on the heating; and their insistence on drying all their washing inside a flat, may well cause or contribute to damp inside the property. Such conduct is likely to give rise to a statutory defence for the landlord. The difficulty will be, however, in proving that such behaviour has taken place – tenants do not tend to advertise that they are causing excessive moisture when inspections take place.

---

15 Section 9A(2)(a).

16 Section 9A(3)(a).

17 There are numerous cases on the meaning of this phrase. For example, behaving in a tenant-like manner includes obligations to clean chimneys when necessary, clean windows; mend fuses; unblocking sinks and plugs; and change washers on taps.

52. Similarly, if, for example, a tenant deliberately breaks the front door of the property so that it becomes unfit (and unsafe) to live in, then the landlord will not be liable because the unfitness has been caused by the tenant's breach of her own obligations.

No obligation to rebuild or reinstate

53. The landlord is not obligated to rebuild or reinstate the dwelling in the case of destruction or damage by fire, storm, flood or other inevitable accident.[18]

Items that may be removed

54. The landlord is not obliged to maintain or repair anything the tenant is entitled to remove from the dwelling.[19] So, if the property is unfurnished and the tenant brings her own furniture, the 2018 Act does not impose any obligations on the landlord in respect of that furniture.

Consent of a third party

55. Another statutory defence is where the required works involve the consent of a third party (for example, a superior landlord or freeholder) and the landlord has made reasonable endeavours to get that consent, but it has not been given.[20] Of course, the meaning of "reasonable endeavours" is likely to be an area of dispute and litigation. The hiring of a private detective to track down an absent freeholder is likely to exceed what is reasonable!

---

18 Section 9A(2)(b)

19 Section 9A(2)(c)

20 Section 9A(2)(e)

56. Nonetheless, landlords should request consents in writing from their landlord or freeholder as soon as practicable and make sure they keep records of these requests. If no response is received, then the landlord should follow up with a further request to protect her position. If a landlord is unable to get hold of the freeholder, or the freeholder simply refuses to engage, then as long as the landlord has made reasonable efforts to make contact, then he will have a statutory defence.

Breaches of other duties or obligations

57. The landlord is not required to carry out works or repairs which, if carried out, would put the landlord in breach of any obligation imposed by any enactment (whenever passed or made).[21] The most obvious example of where this exemption will apply is where the necessary works would involve breaching planning permission.

Summary

- The 2018 Act implies a new term into most residential tenancies
- The term is that the dwelling will be fit for human habitation from the outset of the tenancy and throughout the tenancy term
- The common law rules on notice and/or knowledge are likely to apply
- There is a new right of access granted to landlords in order to allow them to comply with their obligations under the 2018 Act

---

21 Section 9A(2)(d)

- There are a number of statutory defences/exceptions to liability

CHAPTER FOUR REMEDIES AND DAMAGES

1. There are a number of remedies available to a tenant living in a property that is unfit for human habitation. Advisers should consider these options carefully before issuing proceedings.

Interim Injunctions

2. In some cases, it may be possible (or indeed essential) to apply for an interim order forcing a landlord to act. This will mean that the court will hear the application much more quickly; sometimes on the same day that it is issued if the circumstances require. An interim injunction may be sought even before proceedings have been issued. It is also possible to make such an application "without notice" being given to the landlord, although this should only be done in the most extreme and urgent circumstances.

3. If, for example, a property is unsafe and the tenant has nowhere to go, then it may be necessary to apply for an interim order requiring the landlord to make it safe even though the full merits of the case are yet to tested at trial. A tenant considering this option should think carefully before doing so because, ordinarily, the court will require that undertakings be given for the claimant to repay the defendant the costs of complying with the interim injunction if it later transpires that the injunction ought not to have been made.

4. The test to be applied when deciding whether to grant an interim injunction is set out in *American Cyanamid v Ethicon Ltd* [1975] AC 396:

   (a) Is there a serious question to be tried?

   (b) Would damages be an inadequate remedy?

   (c) Where does the balance of convenience lie?

5. An application for an interim injunction will need to be made using the N16A form, which is available to download online. The application will need to be supported by a witness statement setting out the reasons why an injunction is sought and exhibiting any essential documentation or evidence (e.g. the tenancy agreement). If the application is urgent then the applicant will need to (a) request that the matter be listed urgently; and (b) apply for time for service to be abridged if necessary.

Specific Performance

6. The new s.9A(5), Landlord and Tenant Act 1985 provides as follows:

   "Where in any proceedings before a court it is alleged that a lessor is in breach of an obligation under the implied covenant, the court ***may*** *order* ***specific performance*** *of the obligation (regardless of any equitable rule restricting the scope of that remedy)."*

7. So, the 2018 Act makes express provision for the court to order – unfettered by the rules of equity – a landlord to comply with her obligations implied by s.9A. This means that, if at the date of trial, the landlord has failed to remedy

defects that render the property unfit for habitation, the court is likely to make a mandatory order requiring her to carry out the works within a specified period of time. It is worth noting that this power is discretionary (note the permissive use of "may"), so it will be interesting to see if/when or in what circumstances the courts will be willing to refuse to grant specific performance despite making a finding of fact that a landlord is still in breach of her obligations to ensure the property is fit for human habitation.

Damages

8. The 2018 Act works by implying a term into the tenancy agreement, so a tenant's cause of action is breach of contract. As one would expect, a breach of a landlord's covenant to ensure that a property is fit for human habitation will entitle the tenant to recover damages. This book provides a brief outline on this topic, but advisers should consult a practitioner text for more detailed discussion about the principles of damages.

9. Contractual damages are compensatory; i.e. damages are supposed to put the tenant back in the position she would have been in if the contract had been properly performed.

10. General damages and special damages are likely to be available, and the former is likely to be calculated in the same way that damages are already assessed in existing disrepair claims.

General damages

11. In *Wallace v Manchester CC* (1998) 30 HLR 1111 the Court of Appeal approved three different approaches as to how to quantify general damages as follows:

    (a) an award for diminution in the value of the property to the tenant calculated by reference to a proportion of the rent payable;

    (b) a global assessment of discomfort and inconvenience suffered without any reference to the rent payable;

    (c) a combination of an award for diminution in value calculated as a percentage of the rent payable and a separate sum for discomfort and inconvenience.

    It was noted, however, that where the court makes a global award then this ought to be cross-referenced against the rent that was actually payable.

12. More recently in *Moorjani v Durban Estates Ltd* [2015] EWCA Civ 1252 the Court of Appeal confirmed that the underlying principle for all of these methods of assessment is the tenant's "loss of the rights amenity" afforded by the lease as a result of the breach of contract. Briggs LJ provided the following reasoning:

    "Taking those authorities together, I have reached the following tentative conclusions. First, although the language of the Calabar and Wallace cases speak of discomfort, inconvenience and distress as if they were the very losses caused to the lessee by the lessor's breach, the better view is that the loss consists in the impairment to the rights of amenity afforded to the lessee by the lease of which discomfort, inconvenience

and distress (and even the deterioration of the health of a loved one) are only symptoms. The lessee pays a premium for the assignable right to the enjoyment of occupation of a specific property for a period usually longer than his own lifetime, the quality of which is underpinned the lessor's repairing and reinstatement obligations. It is nothing to the point that the lessor incurs no cost in their performance (since that is met either from insurance or service charge). The quality of enjoyment is underpinned by the lessor's promise to carry out those obligations diligently and in due time, rather than to neglect or delay in their performance.

36 Secondly, it is therefore not a fatal obstacle to a claim for damages for that impairment in the lessee's rights that the lessee may have chosen not to make full use, or even any use, of them during part of even all of the relevant period, for reasons unconnected with the disrepair itself. The use which the lessee chooses to make, or not to make, of those rights is, at least in principle, res inter alios acta , in just the same way as the profitable re-letting of premises prior to the quitting of possession by an earlier tenant in breach of his repairing obligations."

13. *Moorjani* is now the leading authority on the principles to be applied when quantifying damages in claims arising from disrepair. Nonetheless, comparator cases are a useful way to advise on quantum and may be used by advocates to persuade the court as to the correct range of damages that ought to be awarded.[1]

1 For this, advisers should consult a casebook, such as *Housing Law Casebook*, Madge, Madge-Wyld.

Special damages

14. Special damages are likely to be available. This means that tenants will be entitled to recover damages representing the loss of items that have been damaged or destroyed as a result of the condition of the property. So, for example, a sum of money would be awarded to account for furniture and clothes that have been destroyed by mould and damp.

15. Tenants should keep a record of all items that have been damaged and keep receipts for the costs of replacing them. The court will usually assess down the cost of brand-new items, under the principle against "betterment" unless it would have been impossible or unreasonable to obtain second-hand replacements.[2]

Failure to mitigate loss

16. The ordinary contractual rules about mitigating loss will apply in cases of breach of the new implied term. In short, it is important that tenants behave in such a way as to limit or mitigate their loss. An obvious example of this is removing furniture from underneath a leak in the ceiling. Tenants who fail to mitigate loss may be subject to a reduction in damages.

Repudiation

17. It is also worth noting that it may be possible for a tenant to treat a breach of the term implied by s.9A as a repudiatory breach of the contract. Thus, it may be possible for a tenant to leave the property before the end of the term having accepted the repudiatory breach of the agreement.

---

2 See *Harbutt's "Plasticine" v Wayne Tank & Pump Co* [1970] 1 Q.B. 447

Summary

- There are a number of remedies available for breach of the new implied term, as follows:

- An interim injunction pending trial (where the facts justify it);

- Specific performance

- General and special damages

- Repudiation of the agreement

CHAPTER FIVE
PRACTICALITIES

Funding for Claims

1. As many readers will be aware, the scope of legal aid was reduced significantly by the Legal Aid, Sentencing and Punishment of Offenders Act 2012 ("LASPO"). Since then, it has only been possible to obtain legal aid for disrepair claims in order to remedy issues causing a serious risk to the health and/or safety of the occupiers. It is also possible to obtain funding to bring a disrepair counterclaim as part of a defence to possession proceedings (e.g. to defeat a claim based on rent arrears). In practice this means that legal aid is only available in the most serious cases where an injunction is sought and does not cover claims for damages. As things stand currently, for claims brought under the 2018 Act, legal aid provision will be available on exactly the same basis as it is for existing disrepair claims.

2. The dearth of legal aid provision means that one of the main alternative ways to fund a claim to enforce rights under the 2018 Act will via conditional fee agreements. These types of arrangements are colloquially known as "no win, no fee" agreements. As one would expect, a CFA allows a claimant to pursue a claim without paying legal fees up front. This approach means that the claimant will only be required to pay their solicitors fees at the end of the claim if it is successful. Lots of solicitors' firms are prepared to act for claimants under CFAs in claims for damages for disrepair. The main requirement for claimants will be to ensure that you meet the solicitors' own internal criteria.

Pre-action Conduct

3. There is an existing "Pre-action Protocol for Housing Disrepair" cases that is used for existing disrepair cases.[1] It can be easily found online on the justice.gov.uk website. At the time of writing the protocol has yet to be amended in light of the 2018 Act. Nonetheless, any changes are likely to be minimal and the existing protocol provides a useful and practical framework for pre-action behaviour that ought to be followed before issuing a claim alleging breach of the new implied term. The court will not be impressed by, and may impose costs consequences on, parties who fail to use the tools available to them.

4. In summary, to comply with the protocol claimants should:

   (a) Consider whether some form of alternative dispute resolution procedure would be more suitable than litigation and if so, try to agree which form to use. The court may require both the landlord and the tenant to provide evidence that alternative means of resolving their dispute were reasonably considered. The types of ADR that might be considered include, mediation, negotiation, and local authority repairs, complaints and/or arbitration procedures. It is important to remember that unreasonable refusal to consider ADR could have cost consequences at the end of proceedings. It may be that a party has entirely reasonable and legitimate reasons to refuse to engage in ADR, but these reasons should be properly explained in correspondence so as to protect that party's position if the issue is raised in the future.

   (b) Send a letter before claim that includes the following information:

1 See para.3 for the scope of the protocol.

i. the tenant's name, the address of the property, the tenant's address if different, the tenant's telephone number and when access to the property will be possible;

ii. details of the defects, including any defects that are yet to be remedied;

iii. provide a brief history of the defects, including any attempts to rectify them;

iv. provide details of any previous notification given to the landlord of the need for repair or explain why the tenant believes that the landlord already has knowledge of the need for repair;

v. set out the effect the defects have had or are having on the tenant and her household (including any personal injury claim by the tenant);

vi. include the identities of all other persons who plan to make a personal injury claim and brief details of their personal injury claims;

vii. give details of any special damages that will form part of the claim;

viii. propose an expert (if necessary and appropriate) and include proposals for the instruction of that expert (perhaps including a draft letter of instruction);

ix. include any relevant documents disclosed by the tenant;

x. make requests for disclosure of documents by the landlord

(c) Wait for a response within a reasonable period of time (usually 20 working days). The landlord should provide a comprehensive response to the letter before claim and a failure to do so is a breach of the protocol (meaning the tenant can issue proceedings).

(d) Where appropriate, instruct a single joint expert to inspect and produce an inspection report. Alternatively, if the parties are unable to agree on a single expert, then it may be appropriate to arrange a joint inspection attended by expert for both sides.

Offers to Settle

5. So many cases of disrepair ought to settle early on but don't. The legal costs in these cases often outweighs the amount of money being claimed. This is because disrepair is a "labour intensive" area of litigation. For example, in a disrepair claim against a local authority, the tenancy file and repairs records may run to thousands of pages. Lawyers will have to wade through this material to find out:

   (a) If, and/or when different individual items of disrepair were reported;

   (b) If, and/or when access to the property was given/denied; and

   (c) If, and/or when repairs were carried.

   This work is slow and often the time spent is disproportionate to the amount of money at stake.

6. Putting in a sensible settlement offer at an early stage is usually a good idea. The potential costs consequences that

flow from a Part 36 offer can be a helpful way of focussing minds and getting the parties to engage with each other.

7. The requirements of a Part 36 offer are technical, and advisers must consult the CPR to check that the strict requirements have been complied with. By way of brief summary, a Part 36 offer must:

    - Be made in writing.
    - Make it clear that the offer is made pursuant to Part 36.
    - Specify a period of not less than 21 days within which the defendant will be liable for the claimant's costs if the offer is accepted, unless the offer is made less than 21 days before the start of the trial.
    - State the scope or extent of the offer in relation to the claim. So, if it relates to a single issue in dispute then this should be made clear.
    - State whether it takes any counterclaim into account.

Expert Evidence

8. Most cases involving unfitness for human habitation will require expert evidence of some sort, but not always. It is entirely possible that the unfitness in a property might be so obvious that a witness statement from the tenant will be enough e.g. lack of heating and hot water in a property is likely to make it unfit for human habitation and no expert report will be necessary at all. Further, in a case of poor housing conditions that have already been remedied, an expert's report will be of no assistance.

9. A HHSRS inspection report carried out by the environmental health department of a local authority, which confirms that there are hazards inside the property will be a very useful piece of evidence to demonstrate that the property is unfit for human habitation. Alternatively, expert evidence may be obtained from a surveyor, engineer, environmental expert or other relevant expert to establish unfitness for human habitation. A surveyor will, ordinarily, make recommendations as to what works are required to remedy the defects and will often include a schedule of works.

10. As noted above, if the pre-action protocol for disrepair claims is followed, then an expert may have been instructed before proceedings are even issued. Advisers should remember that the court must give permission for expert evidence[2] even if the expert was jointly instructed.

Other Evidence

11. Aside from expert evidence there are other equally important matters that must be evidenced to succeed in a claim under the 2018 Act. These matters include: notice of the unfitness being given to the landlord; evidence of causation i.e. evidence that the unfitness alleged caused the damage claimed; evidence of actual loss and damage. Ordinarily these matters can be dealt with in a single witness statement from the tenant.

Which Court?

12. The county court is likely to be the most suitable venue for the vast majority of cases alleging breaches of the new implied

---

2 CPR 35.4

term. In the rarest of cases it may be possible to justify issuing a claim in the High Court where either:

(a) the issues are particularly complex; and

(b) the case is very high in value.[3]

13. If a claim is incorrectly issued in the High Court and then transferred to the County Court there are likely to be significant costs consequences.

Which Track?

14. After a case has been issued it will need to be allocated to one of three "tracks". The scope of each track is set out in detail in CPR 26.6, but, by way of summary:

(c) Small claims track = for the lowest value and most straight forward claims

(d) Fast track = the usual track for modest claims of between £10,000 and £25,000 or claims that are likely to take no more than one day[4]

(e) Multi-track = the track for complex and/or high value cases, which are likely to take more than one day

15. In practice, most disrepair claims end up on the fast track or multi-track because the facts and issues in dispute tend to require at least one day of the courts time. In deciding between the fast track and multi-track the court will consider:

3 Under CPR PD7, para 2.1 provides that proceedings (whether for damages or for a specified sum) may not be started in the High Court unless the value of the claim is more than £100,000.

4 See CPR 26.6 for full

(a) The value of the claim;

(b) The number of witnesses required to give evidence (if it is more than three witnesses then fitting the case into one day is likely to be difficult);

(c) Whether experts will be required to give live evidence; and

(d) The complexity of the law and facts in the dispute.

CHAPTER SIX
HINTS AND TIPS

For Landlords

- Get your house in order quickly! It is now more important than ever to carry out inspections on a regular basis to check the condition of your property. This is crucial when it comes to the common parts because liability in relation to these areas runs from the date on which the defect arises.

- Landlords should make sure that they respond to complaints about conditions quickly and carry out works where required.

- Keep notes and records of conversations, repair works and instances where access had been refused.

- Larger landlords (and in particular social landlords) need to think long-term about estate-wide improvement and repair work projects.

- Social landlords will need to think about updating their policies and procedures for dealing with these issues. Getting advice and working out a strategy early on is likely to be much more cost effective than waiting for claims to be issued.

For Tenants

- Notify your landlord if there are defects in the property as soon as they arise.
- Keep records. It is now easier than ever to take photographs and videos that show poor housing conditions.
- Contact your local authority if you think your property is hazardous – get them to carry out an inspection.
- Get legal advice from a solicitor that has expertise in landlord and tenant disputes.

CHAPTER SEVEN
HELPFUL DOCUMENTS

Example pre-action letter

Dear Sirs,

RE: MR NEVILLE LONGTROUSER, 12 GRIMACE PLACE

We are instructed by your tenant, Mr Longtrouser. This claim relates to the condition of the property occupied by our client pursuant to an assured shorthold tenancy that began on 1 July 2019. We are using the Housing Disrepair Protocol.

Repairs

Our client contends that there are defects in the property that make it unfit for human habitation within the meaning of s.9A, Landlord and Tenant Act 1985. These defects are as follows:

- *Mould and damp in two bedrooms;*
- *Uneven, cracked flooring throughout the kitchen and downstairs bathroom;*
- *A leak coming through the bay window in the living room;*
- *Intermittent heating and hot water as a result of a faulty boiler that routinely cuts out for days at a time.*

History of the defects

The mould, damp and uneven flooring were present at the outset of the tenancy but have gradually got worse over the last three months. Our client noticed the leak through the bay window following heavy rainfall in the first week of September 2019. The issue with the boiler began in mid-July but occasions when it stops working have increased in frequency as the weather has got colder. In total there have been 11 full days during which our client has had no heating or hot water at all.

<u>Notice</u>

Our client has already provided notice in relation to the defects listed above as follows:

- *On 12 September 2019 an email was sent setting out all of these issues and requesting a response;*
- *A telephone call was made, and voicemail message was left, on 16 September 2019;*
- *A property inspection was carried out by your agent on 26 September 2019.*

To date, you have not provided any proposals for remedying these issues.

<u>Impact on our client</u>

The defects at the property are causing significant distress and inconvenience to our client and his household, for example:

- *On 16 September 2019 our client's twelve-year old son fell over in the kitchen as a result of the uneven flooring and grazed his knee;*
- *The intermittent lack of heating and hot water means that our client has had to boil the kettle repeatedly in order to fill a bath for his family to wash;*

- *Our client and his family are having to wear gloves and scarves indoors when the heating is not working.*

Inspection and access

Please arrange to inspect the property as soon as possible. Access will be available on the following dates and times:

- *Afternoon of 1 November 2019*
- *Any time on 3-4 November 2019*
- *Afternoon of 10 November 2019*
- *Morning of 12, 13 and 14 November 2019*

Please confirm by return whether you intend to carry out repairs at this stage or whether you wish to wait until the property has been inspected by the expert as is proposed below.

If you intend to carry out repairs at this stage, please set out a full schedule of intended works including anticipated start and completion dates and a timetable for the works.

Disclosure

Please also provide within 20 working days of this letter all relevant records or documents relating to these issues, including any inventory report that was carried out before our client entered into occupation;

We also enclose copies of the following relevant documents from our client:

- *Our client's tenancy agreement*
- *Email correspondence*

Expert

If agreement is not reached about the carrying out of repairs within 20 working days of this letter, we propose that the parties agree to jointly instruct a single joint expert, Ms Bagshape FRICS, to carry out an inspection of the property and provide a report. We enclose a copy of her CV and a draft letter of instruction.

Please let us know if you agree to this appointment. If you object, please let us know your reasons within 20 working days.

If you do not object to the expert being instructed as a single joint expert, but wish to provide your own instructions, you should send those directly to Ms Bagshape FRICS within 20 working days of this letter. Please send us a copy of your letter of instruction. If you do not agree to a single joint expert, we will instruct Ms Bagshape FRICS to inspect the property in any event. In those circumstances, if you wish to instruct your expert to attend at the same time, please let us know within 20 working days.

Claim

We take the view that you are in breach of your repairing obligations and in particular your duty to ensure that the property is fit for human habitation under s.9A, Landlord and Tenant act 1985 (as inserted by the Homes (Fitness for Human Habitation) Act 2018). Please provide us with your proposals for compensation.

Our client also requires compensation for special damages, and we attach a schedule of the special damages claimed.

Yours faithfully,

Draft letter for the instruction of an expert

Dear Ms Bagshape FRICS

RE: MR NEVILLE LONGTROUSER, 12 GRIMACE PLACE

We act for Mr Longtrouser in connection with a claim arising out of disrepair and poor conditions at 12 Grimace Place, London, EC1 4GW ("the Property"). We are using the Housing Disrepair Protocol.

We would like to instruct you to carry out an inspection and provide a report in relation to the Property. We would be grateful if an inspection could be carried out before 15 December 2019 and thereafter if you could provide a report covering the following points:

- *whether you agree that the defects are as claimed;*
- *whether any of the defects is structural;*
- *what if any risks are presented to the occupiers by any identified defects;*
- *the cause of the defect(s);*
- *the age, character and prospective life of the property;*
- *a schedule of works;*
- *an estimate of the costs of repair;*
- *an assessment about whether you consider it necessary for the occupiers to vacate whilst the works take place.*

Access will be available on the following dates and times:

- *Afternoon of 2 December 2019*

- *Any time on 3-4 December 2019*
- *Afternoon of 10 December 2019*
- *Morning of 12, 13 and 15 December 2019*

You are instructed as a single joint expert.

Please provide the report within 14 days of the inspection. Please contact us immediately if you consider that there are any urgent works that would require emergency repairs and/or an interim injunction.

If the case proceeds to court, the report may be used in evidence. Please ensure that the report complies with Civil Procedure Rules Practice Direction 35.3 and the Guidance for the Instruction of Experts in Civil Claims 2014 at http://www.judiciary.gov.uk.

If you do not have a copy, please let us know.

Yours sincerely,

Draft Particulars of claim

Claim No. 123456

IN THE COUNTY COURT SITTING AT HOGSHEAD

BETWEEN:

MR NEVILLE LONGTROUSER

Claimant

-and-

MR REMUS LUPUS

Defendant

PARTICULARS OF CLAIM

1. *Pursuant to an assured shorthold tenancy that commenced on 1 July 2019, the Defendant let to the Claimant the property at 12 Grimace Place, London, EC1 4GW ("the Property"). A copy of the tenancy agreement is attached at APPENDIX 1.*

2. *At all material times the Defendant has been the freehold owner of the Property and the Claimant's landlord.*

3. *The Property is a two-bedroom, terraced house with a kitchen-diner, one bathroom and a living room.*

4. *At all material times the Claimant has lived at the Property with his partner, Seamus Harrington, and his son, Dean Longtrouser (DOB: 5/5/2007).*

5. *The following are express terms of the tenancy agreement:*

[include any relevant express terms of the agreement]

6. *Further or alternatively, pursuant to s.9A, Landlord and Tenant Act 1985 it was an implied term of the tenancy that the Property was fit for human habitation at the time when the lease was granted and throughout the duration of term of the tenancy.*

7. Further or alternatively, pursuant to s.11, Landlord and Tenant Act 1985 it was an implied term of the tenancy that the Defendant would:

   a. *keep in repair the structure and exterior of the Property*

   b. *keep in repair installations for the supply of water, gas and electricity and for sanitation (including basins, sinks, baths and sanitary conveniences, but not other fixtures, fittings and appliances for making use of the supply of water, gas or electricity).*

   c. *keep in repair installations for space heating and heating water.*

8. *Further or alternatively, pursuant to s.4, Defective Premises Act 1972 the Defendant owed the Claimant and his family a duty to take such care as was reasonable in all the circumstances to ensure the Property was reasonably safe.*

9. *The Defendant has breached the aforementioned terms of the tenancy.*

PARTICULARS OF BREACH

a. *Since the commencement of the tenancy there has been mould and damp in two bedrooms in the Property;*

b. *Since the commencement of the tenancy the flooring in the kitchen and downstairs bathroom has been cracked and uneven;*

c. *From around 6 September 2019 there has been water penetration through the bay window in the living room;*

d. *From around mid-July 2019 the heating and hot water in the property has been intermittent with the boiler that routinely cutting out on numerous occasions for days at a time.*

10. *The Defendant has had notice of these abovementioned breaches*

PARTICULARS OF NOTICE

a. *On 12 September 2019 the Claimant sent to the Defendant an email setting out all of the issues identified in this claim;*

b. *The Claimant called the Defendant and left a voicemail message on 16 September 2019;*

c. *A property inspection was carried out by the Defendant's agent on 26 September 2019.*

d. *On 4 October 2019 the Claimant's solicitors sent a pre-action letter to the Defendant setting out each of the issues raised in this claim.*

11. *By reason of the aforementioned breaches of covenant the Claimant has suffered loss damage, distress and inconvenience.*

PARTICULARS

a. *The smell of mould and damp has pervaded the bedrooms in the Property since the outset of the tenancy;*

b. *Since the commencement of the tenancy the Claimant and his family have had to wear outdoor shoes inside the house as a result of the cracked floor in the kitchen and downstairs bathroom;*

c. *All furniture in the living room has been moved to the centre of the room since water started to penetrate through the bay window on 6 September 2019. The living room has been out of use ever since;*

d. *The Claimant and his family have had to alter their routines each time the hot water has stopped working. This has included having to boil and re-fill the kettle to fill up the bath with hot water so that they could wash.*

e. *When the heating has not been working the Claimant and his family have had to wear multiple layers of clothes inside the house.*

12. *The Defendant has suffered further loss, and claims special damages*

PARTICULARS

a. Water damage to an upholstered three-seater sofa;

b. Water damage to lounge curtains;

c. Numerous items of clothing and linen destroyed by mould.

13. Further, the Claimant claims interest pursuant to section 69 of the County Court Acts 1984 on such damages as are awarded to her at such rate and for such period as the court thinks fit.

AND THE CLAIMANT CLAIMS

1) *An order for specific performance;*

2) *Damages;*

3) *Interest;*

4) *Costs;*

STATEMENT OF TRUTH

(I believe) (the Claimant believes) that the facts stated in these Particulars of Claim are true.

Signed:

Dated:

Full name:

Position

APPENDIX
HOMES (FITNESS FOR HUMAN HABITATION) ACT 2018

(1) The Landlord and Tenant Act 1985 is amended in accordance with subsections (2) to (5).

(2) In section 8 (implied terms as to fitness for human habitation)—

> *(a) in the heading, after "habitation" insert ": Wales";*
>
> *(b) in subsection (1), after "house", in the first place it occurs, insert "in Wales".*

(3) After section 9 (application of section 8 to certain houses occupied by agricultural workers) insert—

> *"9A Fitness for human habitation of dwellings in England*
>
> *(1) In a lease to which this section applies of a dwelling in England (see section 9B), there is implied a covenant by the lessor that the dwelling—*
>
> > *(a) is fit for human habitation at the time the lease is granted or otherwise created or, if later, at the beginning of the term of the lease, and*
> >
> > *(b) will remain fit for human habitation during the term of the lease.*
>
> *(2) The implied covenant is not to be taken as requiring the lessor—*

(a) to carry out works or repairs for which the lessee is liable by virtue of—

(i) the duty of the lessee to use the premises in a tenant-like manner, or

(ii) an express covenant of the lessee of substantially the same effect as that duty;

(b) to rebuild or reinstate the dwelling in the case of destruction or damage by fire, storm, flood or other inevitable accident;

(c) to keep in repair or maintain anything which the lessee is entitled to remove from the dwelling;

(d) to carry out works or repairs which, if carried out, would put the lessor in breach of any obligation imposed by any enactment (whenever passed or made);

(e) to carry out works or repairs requiring the consent of a superior landlord or other third party in circumstances where consent has not been obtained following reasonable endeavours to obtain it.

(3) The implied covenant is also not to be taken as imposing on the lessor any liability in respect of the dwelling being unfit for human habitation if the unfitness is wholly or mainly attributable to—

(a) the lessee's own breach of covenant, or

(b) disrepair which the lessor is not obliged to make good because of an exclusion or modification under section 12 (power of county court to authorise exclusions or modific-

ations in leases in respect of repairing obligations under section 11).

(4) Any provision of a lease or of any agreement relating to a lease (whether made before or after the grant or creation of the lease) is void to the extent that it purports—

(a) to exclude or limit the obligations of the lessor under the implied covenant, or

(b) to authorise any forfeiture or impose on the lessee any penalty, disability or obligation in the event of the lessee enforcing or relying upon those obligations.

(5) Where in any proceedings before a court it is alleged that a lessor is in breach of an obligation under the implied covenant, the court may order specific performance of the obligation (regardless of any equitable rule restricting the scope of that remedy).

(6) Where a lease to which this section applies of a dwelling in England forms part only of a building, the implied covenant has effect as if the reference to the dwelling in subsection (1) included a reference to any common parts of the building in which the lessor has an estate or interest.

(7) In a lease to which this section applies of a dwelling in England, there is also implied a covenant by the lessee that the lessor, or a person authorised in writing by the lessor, may enter the dwelling for the purpose of viewing its condition and state of repair.

(8) The covenant implied by subsection (7) requires entry to the dwelling to be permitted—

(a) only at reasonable times of the day, and

(b) only if at least 24 hours' notice in writing has been given to the occupier of the dwelling.

(9) In this section—

"common parts" has the meaning given by section 60(1) of the Landlord and Tenant Act 1987;

"lease" does not include a mortgage term;

"lessee" means the person for the time being entitled to the term of a lease;

"lessor" means the person for the time being entitled to the reversion expectant on a lease.

9B Leases to which section 9A applies

(1) Section 9A applies to a lease under which a dwelling is let wholly or mainly for human habitation if either of the following applies—

(a) the lease is for a term of less than 7 years, or

(b) the lease is of a kind mentioned in subsection (1A) or (1AB) of section 13 (leases to which section 11 applies: secure, assured or introductory tenancies for fixed term of 7 years or more).

This is subject as follows.

(2) Section 9A does not apply to any lease of a kind mentioned in section 14 (exceptions for leases to which section 11 applies).

(3) Except as mentioned in subsections (4), (5) and (6), section 9A does not apply to a lease granted—

(a) before the commencement date, or

(b) on or after that date in pursuance of an agreement entered into, or an order of a court made, before the commencement date.

(4) Section 9A applies to a periodic or secure tenancy that is in existence on the commencement date, but in the case of any such tenancy the covenant implied by that section has effect in the following way—

(a) subsection (1)(a) of that section has effect as if the reference to the later of the times there mentioned were a reference to the time that begins at the end of the period of 12 months beginning with the commencement date, and

(b) subsection (1)(b) of that section has effect only in respect of times falling after the end of that 12 month period.

(5) Section 9A applies to a periodic or secure tenancy that comes into existence after the commencement date on expiry of a term of a lease granted before that date.

(6) Section 9A applies to a lease for a fixed term which—

(a) is granted or renewed before the commencement date, and

(b) is renewed for a further fixed term on or after that date,

and for this purpose the renewal on or after the commencement date is to be treated as a grant of the lease on or after that date.

(7) For the purposes of subsection (1) it is immaterial—

(a) whether the dwelling is to be occupied under the lease or under an inferior lease derived out of it, or

(b) that the lease also demises other property (which may consist of or include one or more other dwellings).

(8) In determining for the purposes of subsection (1)(a) whether a lease is for a term of less than 7 years—

(a) any part of the term falling before the grant or creation is to be ignored and the lease is to be treated as a lease for a term commencing with the grant or creation;

(b) a lease which is determinable at the option of the lessor before the expiry of 7 years from the commencement of the term is to be treated as a lease for a term of less than 7 years;

(c) a lease (other than one to which paragraph (b) applies) is not to be treated as a lease for a term of less than 7 years if it confers on the lessee an option for renewal for a term which, together with the original term, amounts to 7 years or more.

(9) In this section—

"the commencement date" means the date on which the Homes (Fitness for Human Habitation) Act 2018 comes into force;

"lease", "lessee" and "lessor" have the same meanings as in section 9A;

"secure tenancy" has the meaning given by section 79 of the Housing Act 1985.

9C Application of section 9A to certain dwellings occupied by agricultural workers

(1) This section applies where under a contract of employment of a worker employed in agriculture—

(a) the provision of a dwelling for the worker's occupation forms part of the worker's remuneration, and

(b) the provisions of section 9A (implied term as to fitness for human habitation of dwellings in England) are inapplicable by reason only of the dwelling not being let to the worker.

(2) There is implied as part of the contract of employment (in spite of any stipulation to the contrary) a term having the same effect as the covenant that would be implied by section 9A if the dwelling were let by a lease to which that section applies.

(3) The provisions of section 9A apply accordingly—

(a) with the substitution of "employer" and "employee" for "lessor" and "lessee", and

(b) with such other modifications as may be necessary.

(4) This section does not affect—

(a) any obligation of a person other than the employer to repair a dwelling to which the covenant implied by section 9A applies by virtue of this section, or

(b) any remedy for enforcing such an obligation."

(4) In section 10 (fitness for human habitation)—

(a) the existing text becomes subsection (1);

(b) in that subsection—

(i) after "house", in both places where it occurs, insert "or dwelling";

(ii) after "facilities for preparation and cooking of food and for the disposal of waste water;" insert—

"in relation to a dwelling in England, any prescribed hazard;"

(c) after that subsection insert—

"(2) In subsection (1)"prescribed hazard" means any matter or circumstance amounting to a hazard for the time being prescribed in regulations made by the Secretary of State under section 2 of the Housing Act 2004.

(3) The definition of "hazard" in section 2(1) of the Housing Act 2004 applies for the purposes of subsection (2) as though the reference to a potential occupier were omitted."

(5) In section 39 (index of defined expressions), after the entry in the list for "lease, lessee and lessor (generally)" insert—

"(in the provisions relating to fitness for human habitation of dwellings in England) section 9A(9)".

(6) In section 302 of the Housing Act 1985 (management and repair of houses acquired under section 300 or retained under section 301), in paragraph (c)—

(a) for "section 8" substitute "sections 8 and 9A", and

(b) for "does" substitute "do".

2 Extent, commencement and short title

(1) This Act extends to England and Wales.

(2) This Act comes into force at the end of the period of three months beginning with the day on which it is passed.

(3) This Act may be cited as the Homes (Fitness for Human Habitation) Act 2018.

Explanatory notes

What these notes do

These Explanatory Notes relate to the Homes (Fitness for Human Habitation) Act 2018 (c. 34) which received Royal Assent on 20 December 2018.

- *These Explanatory Notes have been prepared by the Ministry of Housing, Communities and Local Government with the consent of The Honourable Karen Buck MP, the member in charge of the Act, in order to assist the reader in understanding the Act. They do not form part of the Act and have not been endorsed by Parliament.*

- *These Explanatory Notes explain what the Act will mean in practice; provide background information on the development of policy; and provide additional information on how the Act will affect existing legislation in this area.*

- *These Explanatory Notes might best be read alongside the Act. They are not, and are not intended to be, a comprehensive description of the Act.*

Overview of the Act

1. The purpose of the Act is to improve standards in the private and social rented sectors by putting an obligation on landlords to keep their property in good condition and giving tenants the right to take legal action where their landlord fails to do so.

2. The Act is made up of 2 sections and provides that:

- *there is to be an implied covenant in a lease that a landlord must ensure that their property is fit for human habitation at the beginning of the tenancy and for the duration of the tenancy;*
- *and where a landlord fails to do so, the tenant has the right to take action in the courts for breach of contract on the grounds that the property is unfit for human habitation.*

Policy background

3. Landlords are not currently required by implied covenant to ensure that properties they rent out are free of potentially harmful hazards. In the absence of an express term of the lease as to fitness for habitation, an offence is only committed where a landlord fails to comply with a local authority's enforcement notice under the Housing Act 2004. The tenant is unable to take direct legal action to require the landlord to take action for a defective property – they are entirely reliant on the local authority doing so. As a result, it is possible for a landlord to rent out a property which potentially contains a range of hazards caused by the defects and, unless they are formally required by the local authority to rectify them, the landlord cannot be held responsible.

4. The purpose of this Act is to improve standards in the private and social rented sectors by putting an obligation on landlords to keep their property in good condition and giving tenants the right to take legal action where their landlord fails to do so. The legislation will provide:

- *an implied covenant in the lease that all landlords must ensure that their property is fit for human habitation at the beginning of the tenancy and throughout. They should do this by ensuring that their property is free from hazards from which a risk of harm may arise to the health or safety of the tenant or another occupier of the property at the start of the tenancy and keeping it in that condition for the duration of the tenancy; and*
- *where a landlord fails to do so, the tenant has the right to take legal action for breach of contract (covenant) on the grounds that the property is unfit for human habitation. The remedies available to the tenant include an order by the court requiring the landlord to take action to reduce or remove the hazard and/or damages to compensate them for the harm caused by the property which was not fit for human habitation.*

Legal background

5. The Act makes amendments to the Landlord and Tenant Act 1985. Those amendments apply only to England.

Territorial extent and application

6. The Act extends to England and Wales; the new sections 9A-9C of the Landlord and Tenant Act 1985 inserted by the Act will apply to England only. The remaining provisions of the Act apply to England. The existing section 8 of the Landlord and Tenant Act 1985 will continue to apply to Wales.

7. See the table in Annex A for a summary of the position regarding territorial extent and application in the United Kingdom.

Commentary on provisions of Act

Section 1: Fitness for human habitation

8. Section 1(1) provides that the Landlord and Tenant Act 1985 ("LTA 1985") is amended as follows.

9. Section 1(2) amends section 8 of the LTA 1985 to apply only to Wales.

10. Section 1(3) inserts a new section 9A as described below.

9A Fitness for human habitation of dwellings in England

11. Section 9A(1) introduces an implied covenant by the landlord into a lease for the dwelling that the dwelling:

a. *is fit for human habitation at the time the lease was granted;*

b. *will be kept fit for human habitation during the term of the lease.*

12. Section 9A(2) sets out certain exceptions to the application of the implied covenant, in that it does not require the landlord to:

c. *carry out works or repairs for which the tenant is liable because of:*

   i. *the duty of the tenant to use the dwelling in a tenant-like manner, or*

ii. *because there is an express covenant in the lease which requires the tenant to use the dwelling in a tenant-like manner.*

d. *rebuild or reinstate the dwelling where it has been destroyed or damaged by fire, storm, flood or other natural occurrence;*

e. *keep in repair or maintain anything which the tenant is entitled to remove from the dwelling;*

f. *carry out any works or repairs to the property which would result in the landlord breaching any of their statutory obligations under other provisions;*

g. *carry out works or repairs to the property which would require the consent of a superior landlord or other third party, provided that such consent was requested but not obtained.*

13. Section 9A(3) provides that, in addition, the implied covenant does not impose on the landlord any liability where the property is unfit for human habitation where the unfitness is wholly or mainly because of:

a. *the tenant's own breach of the implied covenant, or*

b. *disrepair which the landlord is not required to make good because of an order made by the county court.*

14. Section 9A(4) states that any provision of a lease or any agreement relating to a lease is void where that provision attempts to:

a. *exclude or limit the obligations of the landlord under the implied covenant; or*

b. *authorises any forfeiture or imposes on the tenant any penalty, disability or obligation in the event of the tenant enforcing their rights under the implied covenant introduced through this section.*

15. Section 9A(5) clarifies that where in any court proceedings, it is alleged that a landlord is in breach of their obligation to keep the property fit for human habitation, at the start of and throughout the tenancy, the courts may order specific performance of that obligation.

16. Section 9A(6) states that the duties of the landlord or the lessor extend to common parts of the building where they have an estate or interest.

17. Section 9A(7) clarifies that in a lease of property to which section 9A applies, there is an assumed agreement by the lessee allowing the lessor (or a person authorised by the lessor in writing) to enter the dwelling for the purpose of inspecting its condition and state of repair.

18. Section 9A(8) provides that the landlord, or someone on their behalf, may have access to the property to view its state of repair only if notice is given to the tenant and access is sought for a reasonable time of day.

19. Section 9A(9) clarifies the definitions of the terms "common parts", "lease", "lessor" and "lessee" for the purposes of the provision.

9B Leases to which section 9A applies

20. Section 9B(1) states that the inserted section 9A of the LTA 1985 ("section 9A") applies to a lease under which a dwelling is rented out wholly or mainly for human habitation and:

a. *the term of the lease is less than 7 years, or*

b. *the lease is for a secure, assured or introductory tenancy for a fixed term of 7 years or more.*

21. Section 9B(2) provides that section 9A does not apply to any lease of a type mentioned in section 14 of the LTA 1985.

22. Section 9B(3) states that except as specified in section 9B(4), (5) and (6), section 9A does not apply to a lease granted:

a. *before the commencement date of that section, or*

b. *on or after that date, where the agreement was entered into, or an order of the court made, before the commencement date.*

23. Section 9B(4) provides that section 9A makes provision in relation to a periodic or secure tenancy that is in existence on the commencement date and provides that for such tenancies:

a. *the requirement to ensure the property is fit for human habitation at the time the lease is granted or when it begins is instead a requirement to ensure that it is fit at the time that begins 12 months after the coming into force of section 9A; and*

b. *imposes the covenant to ensure the property is kept fit for human habitation only from 12 months after the coming into force of section 9A. This allows time for compliance in relation to existing tenancies.*

24. Section 9B(5) provides that section 9A applies to a periodic or a secure tenancy that comes into existence after the commencement date on expiry of a lease granted before that commencement date.

25. Section 9B(6) provides that where a lease for a fixed term:

a. *is granted or renewed before the commencement date of this legislation, and*

b. *is renewed for a further fixed term after that date;*

the renewal referred to in paragraph (b) is to be treated as a grant of the lease after that date, at which point the covenant will apply.

26. Section 9B(7) makes clear that for the purposes of the requirement that a property is fit for human habitation at the start of the tenancy and throughout, it is immaterial:

a. *whether the dwelling is to be occupied under the lease or under an inferior lease derived out of it, or*

b. *that the lease also includes other property, which may consist of or include one or more other dwellings.*

27. Section 9B(8) provides that in determining for the purposes of section 9B(1)(a) whether a lease is for a term of less than 7 years:

a. *the lease is to be treated as a lease for a term commencing with the grant of the lease;*

b. *a lease which can be terminated at the option of the landlord before the expiry of 7 years is to be treated as a lease for less than 7 years;*

c. *a lease other than one to which paragraph (b) applies is not to be treated as a lease for a term of less than 7 years if it confers on the tenant an option for renewal for a term which, together with the original term, amounts to 7 years or more.*

28. Section 9B(9) provides definitions to apply in relation to section 9B:

- *"the commencement date" means the date on which the Act comes into force;*

- *"secure tenancy" has the meaning given by section 79 of the Housing Act 1985.*

29. Section 9C restates section 9 of the Landlord and Tenant Act 1985, which will now only apply in relation to Wales.

Remaining provisions

30. Section 1(4) amends section 10 of the LTA 1985. These amendments provide that whether a dwelling is unfit for human habitation is to be determined with regard to a hazard, meaning any matter or circumstance as prescribed in regulations under section 2 of the Housing Act 2004, and that hazard is defined as in section 2(1) of that Act, omitting reference to a "potential occupier". By virtue of the surrounding provisions of section 10, the dwelling shall be regarded as unfit for human habitation if, and only if, it is so far defective in one or more of those matters that it is not reasonably suitable for occupation in that condition.

31. Section 1(5) notes that in section 39 (index of defined expressions), after the entry in the list for "lease, lessee and lessor (generally)" insert "(in the provisions relating to fitness for human habitation) – section 9A(9)"

32. Section 1(6) notes that in section 302 of the Housing Act 1985 (management and repair of houses acquired under section 300 or retained under section 301), in paragraph (c)-for "section 8" substitute "sections 8 and 9A", and for "does" substitute "do".

Commencement

33. Section 2(2) provides that the Act comes into force three months after it has been passed.

MORE BOOKS BY LAW BRIEF PUBLISHING

A selection of our other titles available now:-

'Ellis on Credit Hire – Sixth Edition' by Aidan Ellis & Tim Kevan
'Tackling Disclosure in the Criminal Courts – A Practitioner's Guide' by Narita Bahra QC & Don Ramble
'A Practical Guide to TOLATA Claims' by Greg Williams
'Artificial Intelligence – The Practical Legal Issues' by John Buyers
'A Practical Guide to Prison Injury Claims' by Malcolm Johnson
'A Practical Guide to Hackney Carriage Licensing in London' by Stuart Jessop
'A Practical Guide to Advising Clients at the Police Station' by Colin Stephen McKeown-Beaumont
'A Practical Guide to Antisocial Behaviour Injunctions' by Iain Wightwick
'Practical Mediation: A Guide for Mediators, Advocates, Advisers, Lawyers, and Students in Civil, Commercial, Business, Property, Workplace, and Employment Cases' by Jonathan Dingle with John Sephton
'Planning Obligations Demystified: A Practical Guide to Planning Obligations and Section 106 Agreements' by Bob Mc Geady & Meyric Lewis
'A Practical Guide to Crofting Law' by Brian Inkster
'A Practical Guide to Spousal Maintenance' by Liz Cowell
'A Practical Guide to the Law of Domain Names and Cybersquatting' by Andrew Clemson
'A Practical Guide to the Law of Gender Pay Gap Reporting' by Harini Iyengar
'A Practical Guide to the Rights of Grandparents in Children Proceedings' by Stuart Barlow
'NHS Whistleblowing and the Law' by Joseph England
'Employment Law and the Gig Economy' by Nigel Mackay & Annie Powell
'A Practical Guide to the General Data Protection Regulation (GDPR)' by Keith Markham

'A Practical Guide to Noise Induced Hearing Loss (NIHL) Claims' by Andrew Mckie, Ian Skeate, Gareth McAloon
'An Introduction to Beauty Negligence Claims – A Practical Guide for the Personal Injury Practitioner' by Greg Almond
'Intercompany Agreements for Transfer Pricing Compliance' by Paul Sutton
'Zen and the Art of Mediation' by Martin Plowman
'A Practical Guide to the SRA Principles, Individual and Law Firm Codes of Conduct 2019 – What Every Law Firm Needs to Know' by Paul Bennett
'A Practical Guide to Licensing Law for Commercial Property Lawyers' by Niall McCann & Richard Williams
'A Practical Guide to Adoption for Family Lawyers' by Graham Pegg
'Essential Motor Finance Law for the Busy Practitioner' by Richard Humphreys
'A Practical Guide to Industrial Disease Claims' by Andrew Mckie & Ian Skeate
'A Practical Guide to the Law of Armed Conflict' by Jo Morris & Libby Anderson
'A Practical Guide to Redundancy' by Philip Hyland
'A Practical Guide to Vicarious Liability' by Mariel Irvine
'A Practical Guide to Claims Arising from Delays in Diagnosing Cancer' by Bella Webb
'A Practical Guide to Applications for Landlord's Consent and Variation of Leases' by Mark Shelton
'A Practical Guide to Relief from Sanctions Post-Mitchell and Denton' by Peter Causton
'Butler's Equine Tax Planning: 2nd Edition' by Julie Butler
'A Practical Guide to Equity Release for Advisors' by Paul Sams
'A Practical Guide to Unlawful Eviction and Harassment' by Stephanie Lovegrove
'A Practical Guide to the Law Relating to Food' by Ian Thomas
'A Practical Guide to the Ending of Assured Shorthold Tenancies' by Elizabeth Dwomoh
'A Practical Guide to Financial Services Claims' by Chris Hegarty
'The Law of Houses in Multiple Occupation: A Practical Guide to HMO Proceedings' by Julian Hunt
'A Practical Guide to Unlawful Eviction and Harassment' by Stephanie Lovegrove

'A Practical Guide to Solicitor and Client Costs' by Robin Dunne
'A Practical Guide to Wrongful Conception, Wrongful Birth and Wrongful Life Claims' by Rebecca Greenstreet
'Occupiers, Highways and Defective Premises Claims: A Practical Guide Post-Jackson – 2nd Edition' by Andrew Mckie
'A Practical Guide to Financial Ombudsman Service Claims' by Adam Temple & Robert Scrivenor
'A Practical Guide to the Law of Enfranchisement and Lease Extension' by Paul Sams
'A Practical Guide to Marketing for Lawyers – 2nd Edition' by Catherine Bailey & Jennet Ingram
'A Practical Guide to Advising Schools on Employment Law' by Jonathan Holden
'Certificates of Lawful Use and Development: A Guide to Making and Determining Applications' by Bob Mc Geady & Meyric Lewis
'A Practical Guide to the Law of Dilapidations' by Mark Shelton
'A Guide to Consent in Clinical Negligence Post-Montgomery' by Lauren Sutherland QC
'A Practical Guide to Running Housing Disrepair and Cavity Wall Claims: 2nd Edition' by Andrew Mckie & Ian Skeate
'A Practical Guide to Digital and Social Media Law for Lawyers' by Sherree Westell
'A Practical Guide to Holiday Sickness Claims – 2nd Edition' by Andrew Mckie & Ian Skeate
'A Practical Guide to Elderly Law' by Justin Patten
'Arguments and Tactics for Personal Injury and Clinical Negligence Claims' by Dorian Williams
'A Practical Guide to QOCS and Fundamental Dishonesty' by James Bentley
'A Practical Guide to Drone Law' by Rufus Ballaster, Andrew Firman, Eleanor Clot
'A Practical Guide to Compliance for Personal Injury Firms Working With Claims Management Companies' by Paul Bennett
'A Practical Guide to the Landlord and Tenant Act 1954: Commercial Tenancies' by Richard Hayes & David Sawtell
'A Practical Guide to Psychiatric Claims in Personal Injury' by Liam Ryan
'A Practical Guide to Dog Law for Owners and Others' by Andrea Pitt

'RTA Allegations of Fraud in a Post-Jackson Era: The Handbook – 2nd Edition' by Andrew Mckie
'RTA Personal Injury Claims: A Practical Guide Post-Jackson' by Andrew Mckie
'On Experts: CPR35 for Lawyers and Experts' by David Boyle
'An Introduction to Personal Injury Law' by David Boyle
'A Practical Guide to Claims Arising From Accidents Abroad and Travel Claims' by Andrew Mckie & Ian Skeate
'A Practical Guide to Chronic Pain Claims' by Pankaj Madan
'A Practical Guide to Claims Arising from Fatal Accidents' by James Patience
'A Practical Approach to Clinical Negligence Post-Jackson' by Geoffrey Simpson-Scott
'Employers' Liability Claims: A Practical Guide Post-Jackson' by Andrew Mckie
'A Practical Guide to Subtle Brain Injury Claims' by Pankaj Madan
'A Practical Guide to Costs in Personal Injury Cases' by Matthew Hoe
'The No Nonsense Solicitors' Practice: A Guide To Running Your Firm' by Bettina Brueggemann
'The Queen's Counsel Lawyer's Omnibus: 20 Years of Cartoons from The Times 1993-2013' by Alex Steuart Williams

These books and more are available to order online direct from the publisher at www.lawbriefpublishing.com, where you can also read free sample chapters. For any queries, contact us on 0844 587 2383 or mail@lawbriefpublishing.com.

Our books are also usually in stock at www.amazon.co.uk with free next day delivery for Prime members, and at good legal bookshops such as Wildy & Sons.

We are regularly launching new books in our series of practical day-to-day practitioners' guides. Visit our website and join our free newsletter to be kept informed and to receive special offers, free chapters, etc.

You can also follow us on Twitter at www.twitter.com/lawbriefpub.

www.ingramcontent.com/pod-product-compliance
Lightning Source LLC
LaVergne TN
LVHW022115200926
848481LV00003B/1173
9781912687480